I have sensed our need as a movement to return to a foundation of corporate prayerfulness. Converge exists to glorify God by starting and strengthening churches together worldwide — and our practices need to be undergirded with our prayerfulness. We will accomplish nothing in our own wisdom or power — we are completely dependent on God. The key to our fruitfulness, according to Jesus, is knowing him, abiding in him, connecting with him, relying on him, seeking his will and doing all things in his power and for his glory. True fruitfulness will not happen without true faithfulness in prayer.

Will you join me for the next 21 days in praying for God's leading in our lives, our churches, our movement, our mission fields and our 10-year vision? Will you pray expectantly that God will display his power and faithfulness to us in this season? I believe as we come together, fully submitted to God in prayer, he will display both his person and his power in unprecedented ways. And he will advance the gospel so that more people will meet, know and follow him.

Scott

Scott Ridout,
Converge president

Introduction

"This my God is my prayer. Draw me from Your fire, form me on Your anvil, shape me with Your hands and let me be Your tool." – Max Lucado

Dangerous Prayers! Can prayer be dangerous? Is prayer supposed to be dangerous?

Any encounter with a Holy God can be dangerous—not in a life-threatening way, but in a way that can be life-altering and soul-shaping.

All too often we pray safe prayers: God bless me. God help me. God protect me. God heal me. God provide for me.

Dangerous prayers are risky and life-stretching. Dangerous prayers come out of a spirit of brokenness. Dangerous prayers are filled with boldness and daring faith.

My most dangerous prayers have come in moments of deep frustration and seasons of brokenness. I pray more dangerously when I need to experience God's light in my soul, His power in my ministry, and His leading for the future.

Take Jacob, for instance, who wrestled with God out of great frustration and the paralyzing fear of meeting his brother Esau. He clung to God in prayer as a wrestler grappling with his opponent—and in the process he was changed profoundly *(Genesis 32:22-32)*.

Dangerous prayers:

- Mark our lives. As Jacob was humbled physically, he was reminded that he was also changed spiritually (vv. 25, 31).
- Change our identities. Jacob received a new name, which reminded him that his identity was in God and not in his birthright (vs. 28).
- Draw us closer to God. Jacob came face to face with God. As God's great mercy was revealed, Jacob experienced a deeper sense of intimacy (vs. 30).
- Impact the community of faith. This event in Jacob's life was memorialized to remind us that when a leader is changed, it affects the people they are leading (vs. 32).

Over the next 21 days we are going to explore the dangerous prayers that have been prayed by God's people for thousands of years. We trust God will meet you in a dangerous and life-transforming manner. We pray that you will not be the same and that your family, neighborhood, work place, and church will be impacted because you personally have met with God.

We have broken down these dangerous prayers into three categories:

- Confessional Prayers – "Lord, Search Me"

Confessional prayers allow God to breathe into your life. When you invite His holiness, righteousness, and glory to invade your being, He reveals your needs and any obstacles that are hindering your life and usefulness in His mission.

- Transformational Prayers – "Lord, Break Me"

  Transformational prayers allow God to shape and mold us. They seek God's sanctifying power, strength, and grace as we work out the gospel in our lives through confession and repentance. They seek God's leading by submitting to His Word and surrendering to His ways.

- Missional Prayers – "Lord, Send Me"

  Missional prayers align us with God's purposes. They teach us to rest in God's power and presence as we advance His mission and promote His Glory. They position us to be usable by God in any way possible.

Max Lucado's quote at the beginning of this Introduction refers to God's fire, anvil, and hands. He gives a vivid picture of a blacksmith taking something that is really raw—and with great care and precision, making it beautifully usable.

The first step in God's purifying fire is to invite Him to search us. The next step is to ask God to break us on His anvil, seeking His transformation through shaping and molding us. As the last step, we can then respond to God's call with a willingness to be used as His chosen instrument in His redemptive mission.

This is our prayer: *May God's fire purify your soul. May God's anvil shape and mold your life. And may you become a useful tool, ready to be used in the hands of the Almighty!*

The "Big 5" Prayer Journal

In early 1535, the Protestant Reformation leader Martin Luther was getting his hair cut at the local barbershop. His barber, Peter Beskendorf, asked Dr. Luther this famous question: "Dr. Luther, do you think you could help me learn to pray better?"

Dr. Luther went back to his office and responded with a 40-page letter entitled, How One Should Pray, for Master Peter the Barber. His letter was eventually published as a booklet entitled, A Simple Way To Pray. This timeless booklet has shaped the prayers of God's people for more than 500 hundred years.

Dr. Luther taught his barber how to pray through Scripture, using the example of the Lord's Prayer and the Ten Commandments. He instructed Peter to read or recite Scripture word by word while prayerfully reflecting and asking four questions. These questions were designed to allow God's Word to shape his prayers and take hold of his heart so that he could hear God's voice and submit to His will.

Over 30 years ago, I read Dr. Luther's letter to Peter the Barber. This is one of the most influential teachings ever to shape my prayer life. Building off the foundation of Dr. Luther's wisdom, I have developed what I call "The Big 5 Prayer Journal," based on the following questions:

- What Am I Learning?
- What Am I Thankful For?
- What Do I Regret?
- Who Do I Need to Pray for Today?
- What Do I Need to Do Today?

So How Does It Work?

After reading a Scripture text word for word (one to three times), I prayerfully ask myself the following questions:

What Am I Learning?

What is God teaching me? After prayerfully reading the text I write out some immediate thoughts or lessons that I am learning about God, about myself, and about my relationship with God's mission. If I have time I will do more prayerful study on the text through cross-referencing and word searches around some of the ideas that I sense God is bringing to my attention.

What Am I Thankful For?

This is a time when I glean from the text the various things I learned about God's character and the spiritual blessings He pours out on us. As I write them down, I consciously bring them to God in an act of adoration and worship. I offer them as sacrifices of praise in Jesus' name. William Law wrote, "Prayer is the nearest approach to God and the highest enjoyment of Him that we are capable of in this life."

Worship begins in our prayer closets and breaks forth in corporate worship with other believers. Too often our corporate worship is dry and lifeless because our daily devotion is dull and unmoving.

What Do I Regret?

I then reflect on any sins that are pointed out in the text or during my quietness before the Lord. I confess them by holding them out before God and agreeing that they are wrong, they violate God's holiness, they bring pain to the Holy Spirit, and they hinder the work of God in me and through me. F.B. Meyers wrote, "There are no sacrifices so dear to God as broken hearts; no offerings so precious as contrite spirits."

Who Do I Need to Pray for Today?

This is my intercession prayer list. I write out the names and prayer requests of my family, friends, ministry needs, and goals. Oswald Chambers writes, "True intercession involves bringing the person, or the circumstance that seems to be crashing in on you, before God, until you are changed by His attitude toward that person or circumstance."

He also writes, "Intercession is putting yourself in God's place; it is having His mind and His perspective."

What Do I Need to Do Today?

This is where I write down my to-do list for the day, including projects I'm working on, meetings I will have, phone calls I need to make, and any ministry deadlines and personal goals I need to address. I have learned to pray about everything I do by bringing God into my work. Our work matters to Him! So we need to pray about what we do. As the great devotional writer Oswald Chambers wrote, "Prayer does not fit us for the greater work; prayer is the greater work."

DAILY PRAYER GUIDE

21

Day 1 – Search me, O God!

Psalm 139:23 – Search me, O God, and know my heart! Try me and know my thoughts!

There is no room for morbid introspection in the life of a follower of Jesus. Why? Because when we search our own hearts we can easily fall into self-deception. Jeremiah wrote, "The heart is deceitful above all things, and desperately sick; who can understand it?" He continues, "I the LORD search the heart and test the mind, to give every man according to his ways, according to the fruit of his deeds" (Jeremiah 17:9-10). Only God is qualified to perfectly search our hearts.

David's prayer acknowledges God's searching power, admits that we are so easily deceived, and humbly submits to God's truth rather than our feelings or perceptions.

Find time today to be dangerous! Pray this dangerous prayer:

"Father, I desire to be the best in what I do today. So I ask You to investigate my life and examine my deepest motives. Cross-examine my thoughts and give me a clearer picture of myself according to Your truth. May Your glory be revealed in me and shine through me this day. Amen."

The "Big 5" Prayer Journal

What Am I Learning?

What Am I Thankful For?

What Do I Regret?

Who Do I Need to Pray for Today?

What Do I Need to Do Today?

Day 2 – Teach me Your way, O LORD!

Psalm 86:11 – *Teach me your way, O LORD, that I may walk in your truth; unite my heart to fear your name.*

When we truly love someone, our ultimate goal is to learn what pleases that person. After thirty-five years of marriage I have learned what pleases and displeases my wife. Acting on that understanding has led to joined hearts and a unified marriage.

So it is with true followers of Jesus. They seek to know and live out His commandments in a daily manner so their hearts are united with Jesus and His mission.

David's prayer is a prayer of love—a prayer that seeks to know God's ways and live out God's truth daily for the purpose of uniting our hearts with God's heart.

Find time today to be dangerous by offering this prayer to God:

"Teach me Your ways, O LORD. Train me to walk on Your path of truth, so that my heart will be united with Your heart. I worship You in awe and wonder."

The "Big 5" Prayer Journal

What Am I Learning?

What Am I Thankful For?

What Do I Regret?

Who Do I Need to Pray for Today?

What Do I Need to Do Today?

Day 3 – O God, fulfill Your purposes in me!

Psalm 57:2 – *I cry out to God Most High, to God who fulfills his purpose for me.*

Have you ever wondered why God allows our lives to be overwhelmed with certain problems, pressures, and pain? This is the question behind our prayer today.

David lifted his heart to God, "Be merciful to me, O God, be merciful to me, for in you my soul takes refuge; in the shadow of your wings I will take refuge, till the storms of destruction pass by" (Psalm 57:1).

David is offering a heart cry to God to reveal to him how his personal difficulties can be used to fulfill God's divine purposes. He is begging God to show him how to see God at work even as the storms of life rage against him.

Do you ever feel that way?

The great devotional writer Oswald Chambers wrote, "I have to learn that the aim of my life is God's, not mine. God is using me from His great personal standpoint and all he asks of me is that I trust Him."

Find time today to be dangerous by offering this heart cry to God:

"O God of greatness and goodness, grant me the courage to see everything in my life as a means of fulfilling Your purposes—and not simply my desires."

The "Big 5" Prayer Journal

What Am I Learning?

What Am I Thankful For?

What Do I Regret?

Who Do I Need to Pray for Today?

What Do I Need to Do Today?

Day 4 – Examine me, O LORD!

Psalm 26:2 – *Prove me, O LORD, and try me; test my heart and my mind.*

Just the word examination causes us to tense up. Any type of pop quiz or employee review can put us all on edge.

King David, who was facing a life-threatening event, affirms his trust in the Lord. He declares the integrity of his heart and passionately appeals to God to rigorously examine the truthfulness of all his statements.

David uses three words to reveal the intensity of his appeal: examine, try and test. First, he asks God to examine his intentions, much like a doctor pokes and touches one's body to make sure it is healthy. Second, he appeals to God to smell out (try) his motives like a master chef smells food to make sure that it is fresh and not rotten. Finally, he petitions God to test his heart by putting him through the fire of the furnace, just as precious metals are fired and tested for their purity.

Find time today to be bold like King David and pray this searching prayer:

"O God, let my motives pass your smell test. Examine my life from head to toe and test the purity of my life through Your fire. Amen."

The "Big 5" Prayer Journal

What Am I Learning?

What Am I Thankful For?

What Do I Regret?

Who Do I Need to Pray for Today?

What Do I Need to Do Today?

Day 5 – Teach me to do Your will, O God!

Psalm 143:10 – *Teach me to do your will, for you are my God! Let your good Spirit lead me on level ground!*

Life is sometimes like a treacherous mountain road with deep ruts, dangerous curves, and deadly ravines. If you have ever traveled in remote areas of the world, there is no more relief than to get off that rough, primitive road and onto a smooth, paved, and level highway.

In King David's prayer we discover the essentials in how we can find the level pathways as we travel this life of faith.

The first is a longing to possess an obedient heart. David asked the Lord to teach him how to do His will. David knew that obedience always precedes guidance! Guidance submits itself to obedience. The second is to be in tune with God's Spirit and to experience intimate guidance through the Holy Spirit. David asked God to lead him moment by moment on the level ground in accordance with His loving kindness.

Find time today to seek God's guidance through step-by-step obedience:

"God of all goodness, teach me how to walk in obedience with Your Word and how to be led by Your Spirit so I may find the clear and level path of pleasing You."

The "Big 5" Prayer Journal

What Am I Learning?

What Am I Thankful For?

What Do I Regret?

Who Do I Need to Pray for Today?

What Do I Need to Do Today?

Day 6 – Yes, LORD, I am available and ready to listen!

Exodus 3:4 – When the LORD saw that he turned aside to see, God called to him out of the bush, "Moses, Moses!" And he said, "Here I am."

Moses was 80 years old when God drew him into His service. Our Sovereign Lord used every detail of those 80 years to prepare Moses for this divine moment of surrender. "Here I am" is a dangerous prayer. It is an appropriate response to an effectual call of God. It is a cry of faith. It is that initial moment of surrender that led Moses to grapple with God when he understood the enormity of God's call. Like many leaders, Moses quickly realized that God was calling him to do something way beyond his perceived abilities. When you read Moses' interaction with the Lord in Exodus 3:5–4:17, you see how the Lord carefully, gently, and directly dealt with Moses' objections. Moses ultimately stepped out in faith (Exodus 4:20)—and the rest is history.

When we look back on Moses' life we see he was prepared for this moment because his life was marked with faith (see Hebrews 11:23-28). Day-to-day faith prepares us for big moments of faith. These life-altering moments are the ones that put us dangerously right in the midst of God's mission.

Find time today to pray this missional prayer:

"Father, I am here today, experiencing the wonder of Your presence. I am listening to Your voice and doubting my abilities, but ready to be used for Your glory and the advancement of Your mission."

The "Big 5" Prayer Journal

What Am I Learning?

What Am I Thankful For?

What Do I Regret?

Who Do I Need to Pray for Today?

What Do I Need to Do Today?

Day 7 – Restore my joy and grant me a willing spirit, O LORD!

Psalm 51:12 – *Restore to me the joy of your salvation, and uphold me with a willing spirit.*

The restoration of joy is a daily matter. We live in a world that wants to kill our joy! It wants to rob us of our divine contentment in God's salvation and crush our willingness to obey God in whatever we face.

The first tactic our enemy uses to steal our joy is discouragement. He tries to discourage us through our circumstances of life. He seeks to overwhelm us with the problems, pressures, and pains this world brings. If he cannot discourage us, then his second tactic is to distract us. He tries to conflict us spiritually, morally, and relationally—disrupting our priorities and main focus. And if the enemy of our joy cannot discourage or distract us, then he will seek to derail our faith. His third tactic is to wreck our faith through targeted temptations in the weak areas of our lives. He tempts us to settle for partial obedience or take moral shortcuts.

King David allowed his life to be derailed by sin. But now he cries out to God to restore the wonder of God's forgiveness and salvation. He also petitions God to keep his heart soft, willing, and dependent on Him.

Find time today to pray this prayer of restoration:

"Father in Heaven, overwhelm my soul with the wonder of Your great salvation. Keep my spirit soft, tender, and willing to do Your will this day. Amen!"

The "Big 5" Prayer Journal

What Am I Learning?

What Am I Thankful For?

What Do I Regret?

Who Do I Need to Pray for Today?

What Do I Need to Do Today?

Day 8 – Search my heart for that which offends You, O God!

Psalm 139:24 – And see if there be any grievous way in me, and lead me in the way everlasting!

Self-help psychologists use a technique called the "Johari Window" to help people discover a new level of self-awareness and relational interdependence.

Through a list of adjectives given to both the individual and their peers, they pick the ones that best describe the person. Those they agree on are put in the "Open" category. Those adjectives that are listed only by the individual are put in the "Hidden" category. Those descriptors selected only by their peers are placed in the "Blind Spots" category, and those adjectives not selected by anyone are placed into the "Unknown" category.

When David prays, "see if there is any grievous or painful way in me," he is asking God to reveal to him those "blind spots" or unknown areas of his life that are hindering him from experiencing the fullness of God in his soul and God's pleasing path of blessing.

Find time today to ask God to search you and show you His way:

"Show me, O LORD, my blind spots! Reveal to me, O God, any unknown areas of my life that make me vulnerable. Lead my life on Your right path, Your path of eternal life and infinite blessing."

The "Big 5" Prayer Journal

What Am I Learning?

What Am I Thankful For?

What Do I Regret?

Who Do I Need to Pray for Today?

What Do I Need to Do Today?

Day 9 – O LORD, save me from whining!

Psalm 55:2 – *Attend to me, and answer me; I am restless in my complaint and I moan.*

There is nothing so unattractive as a whiny person. We can have empathy for a person in deep emotional pain. But a whiny person who gets overwhelmed with perceived unfairness and acts like a two-year-old child who did not get his or her way—well, it can be difficult to relate to that person.

And yet, all of us have experienced the embarrassing moment of whining about our circumstances or some unfairness. As soon as we utter that complaint or unpleasant groan, we regret it and want to take it back.

King David catches himself in the same way. With a great level of intensity, he cries out to God in prayer, "Save me from a whiny spirit." His soul was restless because he felt that God was unfair to him, and his spirit was groaning because he was seeking relief.

Find time today to invite God to save you from a whiny spirit in your season of restlessness.

"O God, come quickly. Save me from embarrassing myself. Bring peace to my restlessness and perspective to my pain. Break me of a whiny spirit! Teach me to trust You— and not my circumstances."

The "Big 5" Prayer Journal

What Am I Learning?

What Am I Thankful For?

What Do I Regret?

Who Do I Need to Pray for Today?

What Do I Need to Do Today?

Day 10 – O my God, may my work leave a lasting legacy.

Nehemiah 13:14 – *Remember me, O my God, concerning this, and do not wipe out my good deeds that I have done for the house of my God and for his service.*

There is nothing that grips the human heart so deeply as seeing one's faithfulness and sacrifice produce lasting results. As I get older, the word legacy has a new meaning for me.

Nehemiah answered the call of God. He took great risks and prayed dangerous prayers! God responded by using him to fulfill His purposes. But when Nehemiah returned to see how the work was progressing, his heart was broken! Three times he petitioned God to "Remember me, O God" (vv. 14, 22, 31). Each time he asks God to remember him, we see that his cries grow with a greater level of intensity.

This prayer is dangerous because it asks God to be so intimate with his motives of service that God will not wipe out the work done in his name—but instead establish a legacy of spiritual impact.

Find time today to invite God into your motives for serving Him.

"Father in Heaven, be intimately aware of my motives for serving You so that You will not wipe out my efforts or let others harm the work done in Your name. Father, may You judge my motives and bless the work of my hands for Your honor and glory. Amen."

The "Big 5" Prayer Journal

What Am I Learning?

What Am I Thankful For?

What Do I Regret?

Who Do I Need to Pray for Today?

What Do I Need to Do Today?

Day 11 – Let Your light of truth shine deep within my heart, O LORD!

Psalm 43:3 – *Send out your light and your truth; let them lead me; let them bring me to your holy hill and to your dwelling!*

When we think of light in ancient times, it refers to either the light from a flame or the brilliance of the sun. Both provide illumination, but they can also provide comfort.

God's light not only exposes deep things in our souls, but it also can produce the assurance of warmth. It can illuminate our surroundings, bring clarity to our path, and instill confidence in God's direction.

As we allow the light of God's truth to lead us, it brings us into deeper communion with God and prepares us for corporate worship with God's people. Worshiping God Monday through Saturday is what keeps our worship vibrant on Sunday. "Then I will go to the altar of God, to God my exceeding joy, and I will praise you with the lyre, O God, my God" (Psalm 43:4).

Find time today to be dangerous and invite God's truth to light up your life and ready your heart for worship.

"O LORD, light up my life with Your truth! Shine Your light into the dark places of my soul. Overwhelm me by the warmth of Your loving kindness and draw me in to Your holy presence, for You are my joy. Amen."

The "Big 5" Prayer Journal

What Am I Learning?

What Am I Thankful For?

What Do I Regret?

Who Do I Need to Pray for Today?

What Do I Need to Do Today?

Day 12 – Teach me to number my days, O LORD.

Psalms 39:4-5 – *O LORD, make me know my end and what is the measure of my days; let me know how fleeting I am! Behold, you have made my days a few handbreadths, and my lifetime is as nothing before you. Surely all mankind stands as a mere breath! Selah.*

Billy Graham said, "The greatest surprise in life to me is the brevity of life."

The older I get the shorter life seems. When I look at my children's lives, it feels like life is a flash. One moment I am bringing them home from the hospital, and the next moment I am performing their weddings.

King David invites God to press upon him the shortness of life—and in doing so he discovers the greatness of God and the brevity of man.

Ultimately David's murmurings with God lead him to realizing that his hope is not in this world, but that his hope is centered in God. David writes, "And now, O Lord, for what do I wait? My hope is in you" (Psalm 39:7). Let me paraphrase: "Lord, why am I bothered with the length of my days when my hope is in You?"

Find time today to pray this courageous prayer:

"O LORD, You are my hope! Save me from trusting in my health and my wealth. Keep me centered on You moment-by-moment and day-by-day, for Your glory and the advancement of Your mission. Amen."

The "Big 5" Prayer Journal

What Am I Learning?

What Am I Thankful For?

What Do I Regret?

Who Do I Need to Pray for Today?

What Do I Need to Do Today?

Day 13 – Here I am. Send me, O LORD!

Isaiah 6:8 – *And I heard the voice of the Lord saying, "Whom shall I send, and who will go for us?" Then I said, "Here I am! Send me."*

What happened in Isaiah's life to make him willingly volunteer to be God's man in any tough situation?

First, his heart was changed by the presence of God. God engulfed him with His holiness as he worshipped the Lord in the temple (vv. 1-4). Second, his heart became aware of his sinfulness and his personal need for God's cleansing forgiveness (vs. 5). Third, his heart was broken by the condition of God's people and their need for God's word (vs. 5). Finally, his heart was touched by God's cleansing fire (vv. 6-7).

Accepting God's assignment needs to be rooted in a deep experience with God. God's assignments are miraculous in nature, and only God can change a human heart. Only God can cleanse a sinner and bring revival to a human heart and nation of people.

Isaiah prayed this dangerous prayer because he experienced a dangerous and yet merciful God. Take time today to seek the Lord and listen for His specific assignment for you.

"Holy, Holy, Holy is the LORD God Almighty! Show me the hidden needs of my heart and the brokenness of Your people. Cleanse me, renew me, and strengthen me with the power of Your presence, for I am ready and willing to be used by You for Your great purposes! Amen."

The "Big 5" Prayer Journal

What Am I Learning?

What Am I Thankful For?

What Do I Regret?

Who Do I Need to Pray for Today?

What Do I Need to Do Today?

Day 14 – Make Your face shine upon me, O LORD!

Psalm 119:135 – *Make your face shine upon your servant, and teach me your statutes.*

Do you have memories of your parents or grandparents smiling at you after a big accomplishment such as a good report card, sports achievement, or a musical performance?

The emotion behind receiving approval from others is the emotion behind this prayer. The psalmist is seeking God's smiling approval on his life. He longs for the light of God's countenance and favor to shine on him.

The psalmist wants to experience the High Priest's blessing. "The LORD bless you and keep you; the LORD make his face to shine upon you and be gracious to you; the LORD lift up his countenance upon you and give you peace" (Numbers 6:24-26).

In seeking deeper communion with God, the psalmist is also desirous to learn God's Word and to know God's desires for the sole purpose of pleasing Him.

Dangerous prayers take us to a new level of intimacy in our relationship with God. Take time today to offer this prayer to God:

"Father in Heaven, I live for an audience of one and that is You! Father, I want Your face to shine on my life. May my life be so aligned with Your Word that I will experience Your smiling approval and hear these words from Your heart, 'Well done, good and faithful servant.'"

The "Big 5" Prayer Journal

What Am I Learning?

What Am I Thankful For?

What Do I Regret?

Who Do I Need to Pray for Today?

What Do I Need to Do Today?

Day 15 – Have mercy on me, O God!

Psalm 51:1 – *Have mercy on me, O God, according to your steadfast love; according to your abundant mercy blot out my transgressions.*

Have you ever been spared from what you really deserve?

Driving home late one night after a long day of ministry, I exceeded the speed limit. A State Patrol Officer pulled me over. When he got to the window, I had my driver's license, insurance card, and registration all ready for him. "Sorry officer," I said. "I know I was speeding." He saw my Bible on the car seat next to me and asked, "What do you do?" I replied, "I am a pastor." The officer went back to his car to verify all my information and then came back to the window. He said, "Pastor Rohrmayer, did you know that your driver's license is suspended?" At that moment sheer terror came over my face and panic filled my heart! Before I could say, "What...?" He said, "Gotcha! Slow down next time. Here is a warning."

That is mercy! Mercy is God withholding what we really deserve. Overwhelmed by his sin, King David throws himself on the mercy of God. Dangerous prayers always start with begging God for what we don't deserve.

"O LORD, You know the depth of my guilt! Have mercy on me! Out of Your loving kindness and abundance of mercy, remove from me the stain of my sin, through the precious blood of Jesus my Savior."

The "Big 5" Prayer Journal

What Am I Learning?

What Am I Thankful For?

What Do I Regret?

Who Do I Need to Pray for Today?

What Do I Need to Do Today?

Day 16 – Father, shape me and mold me.

Isaiah 64:8 – *But now, O LORD, you are our Father; we are the clay, and you are our potter; we are all the work of your hand.*

When I was in high school I took a pottery class and learned about the power of the potter's wheel. The potter takes a formless lump of clay, and with strong and steady hands patiently shapes the clay into something useful and beautiful.

Isaiah, out of great frustration, offers this prayer on behalf of himself and God's people. It is a prayer of submission to the goodness of the Father and the greatness of the Potter. A merciful Father will carry us through pains, frustrations, and difficulties of this life, while the Potter's strength can shape those frustrations into something meaningful. Our God is in the soul-shaping business. But transformation will only come through a heart that is surrendered to the Father's love and the Potter's touch.

Be dangerous today and offer this prayer to the Father:

"Take my life, shape it, mold it and conform it.
I yield my life to Your Potter's Hands.
Take my life, use me, lead me and guide me.
I submit my life into Your hands Loving Father."

The "Big 5" Prayer Journal

What Am I Learning?

What Am I Thankful For?

What Do I Regret?

Who Do I Need to Pray for Today?

What Do I Need to Do Today?

Day 17 - Help me finish well, O LORD!

Psalm 71:9 - *Do not cast me off in the time of old age; forsake me not when my strength is spent.*

Many start off quickly, but few finish well. As I move into my 30th year of ministry, finishing well has been at the forefront of my mind.

Tragically, I have seen too many young leaders start the race with wild abandonment, only to disqualify themselves early in the race. Sadly, I have witnessed leaders in the middle years of fruitful ministry fall dramatically and bring shame to themselves and the body of Christ. Appallingly, I have watched leaders end their ministry miserably under the guise of entitlement, forsaking the mission to which they were called.

The first step in finishing the race well starts with pleading for God's favor to do so. In Psalm 71 we see a leader weathered by success and seasoned by failure. He asks God to grant him the spiritual and physical strength to be fruitful as the end of his life is nearing.

Let's be dangerous today. Whether young, old, or in the twilight of life, let's continue seeking God's favor to finish the race of faith courageously.

"Father, as I grow older, may my devotion grow stronger. As my body grows weaker, may Your Spirit strengthen my inner being. Father, grant me the grace to finish well and to continue to be useful in Your service. Amen."

The "Big 5" Prayer Journal

What Am I Learning?

What Am I Thankful For?

What Do I Regret?

Who Do I Need to Pray for Today?

What Do I Need to Do Today?

Day 18 – O LORD, teach me how to treat those who oppose me.

Psalm 27:11 – *Teach me your way, O LORD, and lead me on a level path because of my enemies.*

Choosing the higher road in relationships can be dangerous. But it is the only way God wants us to live. You cannot control the way people treat you, but you can control how you respond to their treatment.

King David was a man who suffered the ill treatment of King Saul. At the time of this prayer, he was running for his life by hiding in caves and retreating into the wilderness. David prayed for God to show him the level path and teach him how to walk on it.

He prayed that God would show the right thing to do in the midst of these unfortunate circumstances. God answered him by saying, "Wait! Wait on me!" (Psalm 27:14).

Waiting on the Lord is courageously trusting God to deal with your enemies. When we learn to wait on the Lord, we find strength to take the high road in our relationships.

Let's be dangerous today by asking God to show us how to take the high road in our difficult relationships.

"O LORD, show me the courageous path to the high road in my difficult relationships! Grant me the strength not to react by taking matters in my own hands, but to courageously wait on You to show me the level path."

The "Big 5" Prayer Journal

What Am I Learning?

What Am I Thankful For?

What Do I Regret?

Who Do I Need to Pray for Today?

What Do I Need to Do Today?

Day 19 – O LORD, grant me truthful lips and a contented heart.

Proverbs 30:7-9 – *"Two things I ask of you; deny them not to me before I die: Remove far from me falsehood and lying; give me neither poverty nor riches; feed me with the food that is needful for me, lest I be full and deny you and say, 'Who is the Lord?' or lest I be poor and steal and profane the name of my God."*

Honesty and contentment are the pathways that lead to a life of integrity and generosity. Removing falsehood includes forsaking exaggeration, abandoning partial truths, and seeking to be truthful in all situations.

Finding contentment is really about the experience of satisfaction. What ultimately satisfies you? If your satisfaction comes from material wants, you will eventually feel empty. If these cravings go unchecked you can end up doing crazy things to meet them and hurt yourself in the process (Proverbs 23:4-5).

In this short but dangerous prayer, Agur invites God into his private world, the world of his thoughts, and needs of his soul for the purpose of aligning his heart to bring pleasure to God.

"O God, I beg two favors from you; let me have them before I die. First, help me never to tell a lie. Second, give me neither poverty nor riches! Give me just enough to satisfy my needs. For if I grow rich, I may deny you and say, 'Who is the Lord?' And if I am too poor, I may steal and thus insult God's holy name" (Proverbs 30:7-9, NLT).

The "Big 5" Prayer Journal

What Am I Learning?

What Am I Thankful For?

What Do I Regret?

Who Do I Need to Pray for Today?

What Do I Need to Do Today?

Day 20 – Yes, Lord, I am listening!

Acts 9:10 - *Now there was a disciple at Damascus named Ananias. The Lord said to him in a vision, "Ananias." And he said, "Here I am, Lord."*

Hearing God's voice can be a dangerous proposition. Ananias received a vision from God and his first response was, "Here I am Lord." He was open and willing to do the Lord's bidding. And yet when he found out what the assignment was, he hesitated and questioned the Lord (Acts 9:11-14). I don't think this reflects Ananias' lack of faith as much as it reveal Saul's notorious reputation.

So many times we get the call of God, but then we run into walls of difficulty that test our commitment to the call. This is what leaders call a crisis of belief. It is that moment when our faith is tested and our true belief in God is revealed. God does not expect blind obedience. He has called us into a relationship, and through that relationship we wrestle with His missional purposes as they are worked out in our lives.

In the end Ananias trusted God and brought God's message to Saul (Acts 9:17-19). It all started with a dangerous prayer, "Here I am, Lord."

"Here I am, Lord. I am open, ready, and willing to do what You ask of me. Grant me the courage and conviction to see beyond the obstacles, to rest in Your promises, and to see Your mission fulfilled through me. Amen."

The "Big 5" Prayer Journal

What Am I Learning?

What Am I Thankful For?

What Do I Regret?

Who Do I Need to Pray for Today?

What Do I Need to Do Today?

Day 21 – Lord, increase my faith!

Luke 17:5 – *The apostles said to the Lord, "Increase our faith!"*

Have you ever been pushed to your limit spiritually, emotionally, intellectually, and relationally? This is what devotional writers call brokenness. Brokenness is when you realize that you are completely powerless to achieve God's highest ideals, and you humbly throw yourself on God's mercy. Dangerous prayers are birthed out of seasons or moments of brokenness.

Pressed to the wall with what seemed to be an impossible challenge of offering unlimited forgiveness to a repentant offender (Luke 17:1-4), the apostles acknowledge the impossibility and prayed a dangerous prayer: "Increase our faith!"

God wants His children to live in utter dependence on Him. The Bible says, "we walk by faith, not by sight" (2 Corinthians 5:7). In that moment of brokenness the apostles chose faith rather than reason. In fact, they offered the only thing they had—their faith. They asked the Author of their faith to increase it so that they could see God do the impossible!

Today let's be dangerous and ask God to increase our faith.

"Father, I'm at my wits' end! I can't do what You are asking in my own strength! I need You. I need Your strength and I need You to increase my faith to see You work supernaturally in my life and ministry. Father, I believe, but help me overcome my unbelief. Amen."

The "Big 5" Prayer Journal

What Am I Learning?

What Am I Thankful For?

What Do I Regret?

Who Do I Need to Pray for Today?

What Do I Need to Do Today?

✝ CONVERGE

Converge is a movement of churches working to help people meet, know and follow Jesus. We do this by starting and strengthening churches together worldwide.

For over 165 years we've helped churches like yours bring life change to communities in the U.S. and around the world through church planting and discipleship multiplication, leadership training and coaching and global missions.

We are rooted in the gospel and the infallible, inerrant word of God and the need for every person to surrender to Jesus for salvation. Our goal is to give every person the opportunity to hear the gospel, say "yes" to Jesus, grow in faith, be equipped to serve and be sent out. We are committed to seeing vibrant churches in every community, state and country within our reach. We want every person to experience a life-changing, personal relationship with Jesus.

Our churches come together around something greater than a compelling mission. What brings us together is Christ's completed work on the cross. Because of the cross, we have forgiveness from our past, power for our present and hope for our future. As a result, we converge around the cross to take what Christ has done for us and make it known to others.

Throughout our history we have seen generations of churches, leaders and missionaries join forces through God's power to accomplish the impossible. His command to go and make disciples resonates in our hearts and churches. It is evident in the ministries of our congregations and mission fields.

As we continue to move forward, we are asking God to help us:

Open the front door to see more churches started, disciples multiplied and missionaries sent out.

Close the back door to develop more healthy, growing churches and leaders.

Tear down the walls to expand our cultural diversity and address racial barriers to advance the gospel.

Build the house to increase collaboration and resources needed to start and strengthen more churches.

We believe this emphasis will result in more followers of Jesus—who are focused on the mission of Jesus.

Learn more about Converge at converge.org

About the author: Gary Rohrmayer

Gary Rohrmayer was born in Waukesha, Wisconsin. Growing up in a family of entrepreneurs, he turned his entrepreneurial energy into starting new churches throughout the Midwest after experiencing a dramatic conversion. As a pastor, author, speaker, coach, trainer and leader, he has a unique focus in mobilizing and mentoring leaders in the mission of Jesus. He specializes in equipping leaders in areas of spiritual formation, church planting and church health. Gary has been a force in church planting since 1987. During this time, he has been involved in over 171 new church plants and trained thousands of church planters across the country. He currently is serving as the president and executive minister of Converge MidAmerica, overseeing its business and ministry interests that support regional church planting and ongoing care of its partner churches. Gary's vision is to see "that no leader travels their ministry journey alone." Gary and his wife, Mary, have three grown children and live in the greater Chicago area.

Check out other resources designed to reignite your prayer life and strengthen your relationship with God and His mission.

21 Days of Prayer and Fasting: A Fasting Guide for Spiritual Breakthroughs

In the 21-day journey, Gary Rohrmayer introduces you to the rich spiritual discipline of fasting through the holy scriptures and the great Christian thinkers throughout the ages. Our prayer is that your passion for God will lead you to the breakthroughs you are seeking personally and for your church.

21 Courageous Prayers: A Transformational Journey for Moving from Fear to Faith

In 21-day journey, Gary Rohrmayer introduces you to the spiritual discipline of reading, meditating on, and praying through the book of Psalms. Our hope is that God will infuse your heart with a courageous faith and fill your mouth with courageous prayers as you trust His promises, rely on His power, and experience His presence.